Praise for Stephanie Braun Orfali's previous book
A Jewish Girl in the Weimar Republic :

"Touchingly recreates the joys, the tragedies, the daily routines and ultimate fate of her family . . . most engaging characters."
   -- Publishers Weekly
"A loving personal rememberance of innocence."
   -- Choice
"A delightful autobiography describing the life of Stephanie Orfali in Nuernberg."
   -- Aufbau
"Paean of praise for the assimilated Jews who were in the vanguard of the sophisticated international culture which flourished in Germany till Hitler."
   -- Jerusalem Post
A vivid picture of the rich cultural life in [Nuernburg] . . . poignant autobiography."
   -- KLIAT Young Adult Paperback Book Guide
" honest, chatty style . . . Orfali's factual memoir about her colorful family helps fill the gap in Holocaust literature."
   -- Small Press
"Captures a teenager's feelings trying to understand a world in turmoil . . . A personal history of Orfali's roots from the late 1800's to 1934, describing how her family life was affected by the impending rule of the Nazis."
   -- Northern California Jewish Bulletin
"Vividly and unforgetably evokes her childhood in the Bavaria of the 1920's . . . a penetrating and subtle analysis of her family's psychohistory."
   -- The Express
"Includes intimate notes about her family and friends, and her romances as a young woma
   -- The Napa Regist
"A revealing family history."
   -- Napa Valley Time

T0161307

Young Steffi during her first year in Eretz Israel.

A Jewish Girl Finds New Roots

by Stephanie Braun Orfali

Ronin Publishing, Inc • Berkeley, CA

A Jewish Girl Finds New Roots
ISBN: 0-914171-91-7

Editors: Sebastian Orfali, Gabrielle Scaccia, Jacob Orfali,
        Wolfgang Braun, Beverly Potter, Frank Scaccia
Design: Sebastian Orfali, Candy Avila
Typing: Gabrielle Scaccia, Renate Busse, Candy Avila
Translations from German: Renate Busse

Published and Distributed by:
RONIN PUBLISHING, INC.
Post Office Box 1035
Berkeley, California 94701

First printing 1997

9 8 7 6 5 4 3 2 1

Printed in the United States of America

Dear readers,
family and friends,

We have before us a treasured legacy, which my sister Steffi, of blessed memory, left for us to get some insight into her personal life. She surely was endowed with a searching mind, all the time inventing and active.

So she engaged herself in her last year with writing a biography, looking back into her past, tumultuous as it was all along. The project was unfortunately still unfinished, only in haphazard and fragmentary array. Yet enough to get a glimpse of her outlook on life. It reveals to us her unfailing mastery in combating hardships, solving problems and enjoying the brighter sides too.

As death came to her suddenly and unsuspected, this document keeps her alive in our hearts with a vivid touch.

Brother Floh Braun

August 1996

Preface

One very busy day while shopping with my mother, she handed me a short story written by my Grandmama. I was too busy looking through the sale table for a winter hat to pay attention. Grief was in control, not me.

Despite the resistance, I chose a black stocking cap for $1.99. Mom found some lemons for $2.99 and threw them in the cart. Quite a bargain, I thought quietly to myself. The five typewritten pages found their home under my arm and we were shortly on our way.

I still remember the sound of voice of Oma's saying an old adage that if life hands you lemons, one is to make lemonade.

I remember some old stories of my now departed Oma. She spoiled me rotten and I am eternally grateful. I saw her hometown of Nurnberg when I was a mere 17 years old. Just a lad, riding down the Rhine. Reading "The Teeth of Polycrates" reminds me of her kindness and sense of adventure.

The poems are full of sadness, but the reader must remember that she was a survivor and had a hard life. I urge one to notice the mention of God and also to take note of the sarcastic tone. This is the only way that the color of the stories will shine through the layers of hardship that Steffi faced every day and the cancer which eventually took her life.

When my Oma died, it came as quite a shock to me. I already had one other grandmother withering away before my eyes in my childhood home, also from cancer. God handed me a plate of big red fat sour lemons. As you know, that is the wrong color for that fruit.

Due to the Sweetness and kindness of God, I now can deal with the loss and I can again contribute to humanity in ways I never dreamed possible. Thank you Steffi for being such a good teacher to your little grandson Frankie.

I never bade a fond farewell to my sweet Grandmother Orfali. I guess it just wasn't in the plan. If you choose to read on, forgive the author's ":cherman:" accent. Understanding the imagery will be easier if you take my advice - grammar rules are only for the persnickety.

Have fun with this book.

If you cannot read, then have someone else do it or ask me for the voice-over tape which accompanies the manuscript. Death cannot squelch the voice of a strong woman, and Oma was the strongest person I ever knew. And thank you for teaching me how to make the perfect glass of lemonade.

I loved you very much,
your grandson,
Frankie.

Contents

Selected Poems
by Stephanie Orfali

Vorbei

Du sahst mich an mit so leerem Blick
Und hast mich doch einmal lieb gehabt.
Jetzt liegt mein Herz zertreten am Boden und weint
Weil ich Dir fremd geworden bin.

It's Over

You looked at me with such an empty glance
And yet you loved me once
Now my heart lies trampled on the ground and weeps
Because I became a stranger to you

(1934)

Starry Night

I wish I were akin to you, oh starry night.
You are so clear, so mild, so pure.
You stretch your silver hand to cover
grief, sadness, and despair.
You comfort weary souls as mothers do.
Your golden stars are weaving shiny veils
That unify the universe and show
the unity between us mortals and the galaxies.

(Translation of a poem written during 1934, my first year in Israel)

Das Leben

So liegt's vor mir, mein Leben.
Was wird es mir wohl geben?
Ein Wuerfelspiel ist's noch
Und zwingen muss ich's doch.
Und denk ich an eas Ferne,
O Gott, ich tu's nicht gerne,
So droht es finster, duester, hart.
So ist es kalt und boeser Art
Nur wenig Freude und viel Harm
Und kaum ein Tag voll Liebe warm.
Es ist ein Leben, wie alle es fuehren
Geschehen, die taeglich ans Herz uns ruehren
Und trotzdem Leben und doch kein Tod,
Was laesst uns leben in diesser Not?
Es ist nicht nur Hoffnung
            auf kuenftiges Glueck
Es ist nicht nur Angst vor dem
            Nimmerzurueck.
Es ist das "Gute", was uns haelt
Es ist das Edle in dieser Welt
Ich weiss: sind auch die Menschen schlecht,
Sie kennen das Gute und erkennen's
            als recht.

(3 Dez 1929)

Life

So it spreads out before me, my life.
What will it give me?
A game of dice it is still
And I must force it nevertheless.
And thinking of the remoteness
O God, I do not like it
So darkly threatening, obscure, hard
It is so cold and of malevolent kind
Only little joy and much grief
And hardly a day of warm love.
It is a life as all are leading it
Happenings which daily touch our hearts
And still it's life and not yet death
What lets us live in this sorrow?
It is not only hope for future bliss
It is not only fear of the no-return
It is the "goodness" that holds us
It is the worthiness of this world.
Even if mankind is depraved
They know the good and recognize it
        as right.

(3 Dez 1929)

Unser Glueck

Lass Sorgen und Jammer
Daheim in der Kammer!
Jauchz' mit in das Leben!
Es braucht Dir nicht geben
    Das Glueck.
Du hast's ha gewonnen
Du hast ha die Sonnen
Gar fest im Herzen.
Was machst Du Dir Schmerzen?
    Ums Glueck.
Es toenet und singet,
Es jauchzet und klinget
Im Zweiklang in Dir:
So komm doch mit mir
    Ins Glueck.
Betreten ist zwar jeder Steg
Begangen ist zwar jeder Weg
Doch werden wir alle ueberholen
Wir wandeln ja auf leichten Sohlen.
    Auf Glueck1
Ich gehe mit ins Weite
Ich gehe mit zum Streite
Wir haben vor uns der Arbeit viel
Du hast Dir gesteckt ein hohes Ziel
    Voll Glueck.
Wir werden nicht weichen.
Wir werden's erreichen.
Durch unser Leben
Den andern zu geben
    Sei unser Glueck.

Our Happiness

Leave sorrow and lamentations
At home in your chamber
Exult in life
It does not have to give you happiness.
You have won it.
You have the sun
Strongly anchored in your heart
Why give yourself pain?
For happiness
It sounds and sings
It exults and rings
In dual harmony in you
So enter with me
Into Happiness
Strolled along, indeed, is every path
Walked upon, indeed, is every road
Yet we will overtake them all
We stride along on nimble-footed soles
       Toward bliss!
I go along to the horizon
I follow to the fight
We have much work to do.
You have set yourself a high aim
Much luck
We will not give in
We will achieve it.
Through our life
To give to others shall be our happiness.

(Summer 1928)

Mutter

Ein Herze schlaegt
     fuer Dich, fuer Dich!
Ein seele fuehlt
     fuer Dich, fuer Dich!
In Freud und Leid
fuehlt sieh mit Dir.
Warst eins mit ihr
     und bist es noch.
Moegst Du es immer bleiben!
Hast Du zu klagen,
     sie versteht's
Sie ist Dein Treustes
     jetzt und stets/
Und kommt die Liebe,
     reisst Dich fort
Es bleibet Dir
     ein fester Hort:
     Das Mutterherz.

Mother

A heart beats
     for you, for you
In joy and sorrow
     it (she) feels with you.
You were as one with her
And are so still
May you always remain so!
Have you complaints
     She understands
She is your truest (friend)
     now and ever.
And comes love,
Tears you away
It stays with you
     a strong keep,
The heart of a mother.

Meiner Mutter zum Geburtstag

Wieder nahn mit besten Wuenschen
    alle Deine Lieben sich.
Wieder ist ein Jahr verflossen
    und wir feiern Dich.
Alle, alle kommen gerne
    um zu sagen wie so sehr
Unsere Mutter sie verehren
    Willst Du da noch mehr?
Sieh! Wir alle lieben Dich,
    wuenschen Dir das Best
Und uns alle hast bei Dir,
    hier, daheim, im Nest.
Hast uns gegeben
    das Best auf der Welt:
Ein Elternhaus
    das uns allen gefaellt.
Du hast Deinen Kreis
    von Liebe voll.
Weiss kaum was ich Dir
    noch wuenschen soll.
Ein' heitern Sinn,
    ein frohes Herz,
Recht viel Gesundheit,
    niemals Schmerz.
Ein' jungen Geist
    Dein Leben lang,
Dann ist mir um Dein Glueck
    nicht bang.

(Ende Mai 1927)

For My Mother on Her Birthday

Again are approaching with all best wishes
     all your loved ones.
Again a year has passed
     and we are celebrating you.
All, all are happy to come
to say how very much
Our Mother they honor.
Can you wish for more?
Look, we all love you
     with you all the best
And you have us all with you
here, at home, in the nest.
You gave us the best in the world
a home that all of us love.
You have your circle
full of love.
I hardly know what I still
     should wish for you.
The best of health
     never pain.
A cheerful mind
     a happy heart
The best of health
     never pain
A young spirit
     all your life long
Then I won't worried about your happiness.

(End of May 1927)

Sehnsucht

Du bist so fern
Du bist so weit
Wie draengt es mich
Die ganze Zeit
    Zu Dir.
Ich denk' an Dich
Ich denk' zurueck
An schoene Stunden
Voller Glueck
    mit Dir
Nicht aus ist
Diese schoene Zeit
Nicht sind die
Stunden mehr so weit
    bei Dir.
Bald bist Du da
Bald wird es gut
Ich denke dran
Mir waechst der Mut.

(August 1928)

Longing

You are so far
You are so distant
How much I long
All the time
        to be with you.
I think of you
I do remember
The happy hours
Full of bliss
        with you.
Not yet over is
This happy time,
Nor are the
Hours so far apart
        From you.
Soon will you be here
Soon it will be good
I think of it
My courage grows.

(August 1928)

Gott

O Gott, verbirg Dich nicht so fern.
Du bist doch da, ich weiss es ja.
Warum laesst Du Dich nicht erkennen?
Huellst alles ein in tiefes Schweigen,
Laesst nicht einmal uns selbst uns eigen?
Laesst elle fragen nur "warum"
Und uns auf Antwort warten?
Ich kann nicht mehr, es ist zu schwer
Es sind zu viel der Fregen um mich her.
Wast ist der Mensch? Was tut er da?
Wozu das Leid? Warum die Sonne?
Warum verbirgst Du Dich so fern?

(Ende Juni 1928)

God

O God, don't hide from me so far
You are still there, I know it.
Why don't you let me know you?
All is covered in deep silence
You don't ever let us be ourselves
You only let us all ask "why"
And let us wait for an answer?
I cannot go on, it is too hard
There are too many questions about
What is man? What does he here?
Why the suffering? Why the sun?
Why do you hide so far?

(End of June 1928)

Hoffnung

Leben, Lachen, Lieben
Sind ja noch geblieben
Sind nicht mit gestorben
Als die erste Lieb verdorben.
Schliefen nur die lange Zeit
Und sind immer noch bereit.
Leben, Lachen, Lieben
Sind ja noch geblieben
Tanzen weiter, muntre Reih'n
Frohsinn kehrt ins Herze nein
Und drum fort so machn:
Leben, liebn, lachn.

(September 1928)

Hope

Life, laughter, love
Are still with us,
Have not died
When the first love floundered.
They were only asllep all this time
And are still there.
Life, laughter, love
Are still with us,
Dancing on in lively rows.
Cheerfulness returns to my heart
And therefore I continue to
Live, love, laugh.

(September 1928)

Tausend

Tausend Herzen schlagen nach Glueck
Tausend Seelen traeumen vom Glueck
Und tausend Menschen rissen einander
Lebend das zuckende Herz aus der Brust.
Tausend Sterne erhellen die Nacht
Tausend Lichter ergluehen in Pracht
Und tausend erzittern
     bange im Licht.
Tausend Worte hab ich gesagt
Tausend Fragen hab ich gefragt
Und tausandmal sagte ich "nein"
     und war betruebt.

(Februar 1933)

A Thousand

A thousand hearts beat for happiness
A thousand souls dream of bliss
And thousands love from each other
Living the jolting heart from the breast.
A thousand stars light up the night
A thousand lights glow in splendour
And a thousand trees tremble
     frightened in the light.
A thousand words have I exclaimed
A thousand questions have I asked
A thousand times did I say "no"
     And was sad.

(February 1933)

Lebensfreude

Ich liebe dich, Leben, in Deiner berueckenden Kraft.
Ich liebe Dich, Natur, die schafft.
Ich freu' mich des Fuehlings, der lachenden Baeume
Ich freu' mich der bunten, verwirrenden Traeume.
Bin gluecklich, dass ich mein Leben lenke
Bin gluecklich, dass ich fuehle und denke,
Und dass ich feine Menschen kenne,
Dass ich sie meine Freunde nenne.
Ich moechte allen davon geben
Von meiner Liebe zum vollen Leben.

(27 April 1931)

Love of Life

I love you, life, in Your enchanting power
I love you, nature, the creator
I am gladdened by Spring's laughing trees
I am enjoying the colorful perplexing dreams
Am happy that I livest my life
Am happy that I feel and think
And that I know fine people
That I can call them my friends.
I want to give to all
Of my love for a full life.

(April 27, 1931)

Abend

Wir haben uns muede geschafft.
Es war ein heisser Tage wie all Tage
und dann kam schnell die dunkle Nacht herein
und ich sitze im Wind.
Am zerissenen Himmel stehn Waolken und Sterne.
Was da im Dunkel liegt is
Unsere Erde und grosse sehnsucht
Ist in mir zu dieser Erde die
Wir am Tag hart angefasst mit unseren Haenden.
Es liegt das ganze Werk im Dunkel eingebettet.
Ein wilder Wind weht ueber uns hinweg.
Und das Gesicht dem Winde zugewendet stehen wir.
Wird es gelingen, das Werk?

(1934)

Evening

We exerted ourselves until fatigued
It was a hot day like all days
And then rapidly came the dark night
and I sit in the wind.
On the newborn sky are the clouds and the stars
What lies there in the darkness is
Our earth, and a great craving
Fills me for this earth which during
The day we touched roughly with our hands.
The whole work lies embedded in darkness
A wild wind blows over us.
And the face burned towards the wind we stand.
Will it succeed, the work?

(1934)

Tod

Und Vergessen wird sein
Eine ungeheure Leere wird uns umschlingen und
Seeligkeit tiefen traumlosen Schlafes wird sein.
Alle Schmerzen, alles Sehnen wird ausgeloescht sein
Und tausendfach Ruhe wird unser Trost sein.
Wann, wann wird die Erloesung kommen
und wieviel Leid muss
ich noch vorher trinken bis ich
die Ruhe mir erkauft.

(1934)

Death

And oblivion will be
An immense emptiness will embrace us
And blissfulness of deep dreamless sleep will be.
All pain, all longing will be exhausted
And thousandfold rest will be our consolation.
When, when will the redemption come
And how much grief must I still drink
Before I procure my rest.

(1934)

Noch ist es die Nacht

Noch ist es die Nacht
Noch ist es die Nacht die beklemmende
      angstvolle Stille
Noch ist es die Nacht die uns bange
      erzittern heisst
Noch haelt uns beherrscht ein fremder
      Wille
Noch fuehl ich die Qual, die das Herz
      zerreist
Noch ist es die Nacht
Noch sind es die Sterne
Noch ist es der Rausch
Noch ist es der Wein
Noch taskten wir zoegernd,
Noch ahnen wir ferne
Noch sind wir klein
Noch ist es die Nacht
Die Sehnsucht, der Krampf
Wir kennen von fern nur
den sieghaften Kampf.
Noch ist es die Nacht
Sie beherrscht unser Leben
Noch ist er ferne der Tag das Streben
Das Streben nach Arbeit und Klarheit und Kraft.
      Auf Israel, baue Dein Land.

(15 Oktober 1934)

It is Still the Night

It is still the night.
It is still the night, the oppressive, fearful silence.
It is still the night which makes us tremble.
We are still dominated by a strange will
And I feel the torment which tears at the heart.
It is still the night.
It is still the stars.
It is still the intoxication,
It is still the wine.
We still touch hesitantly,
And anticipate from afar.
We are still small,
It is still the night,
The longing, the spasm.
We know only from afar
The victorious fight.
It is still the night
That dominates our life.
It is still fear, the day and the effort,
The striving for work and certainty and strength.
Onward Israel, build your land!

(October 15, 1934)

Alltag

Der kleine Alltag ist so grau
Man sieht nicht auf
Und haelt den Kopf gesenkt
Man geht gebueckt im Kreis und stiert
Und zaehlt bis tausend,
Nur dass man nicht denkt.
Der kleine Alltag ist erfuellt
Von tausend Wuenschen, hoffnungslos und klein
Er ist erfuellt von Haesslichkeit und Neid
Von Zwielicht und von Muedesein.
Der kleine Alltage ist voll Bangigkeit
Er ist wie kalter Zigarettenrauch
So oed und fad und dumpf dabei.
Doch voll Erinnerungen ist er auch.

Everyday

The small everyday is so gray
One doesn't look up
And keeps one's head down
One walks bent down in circles and stares
One counts to thousand
Only not to think.
The little everyday is filled
With thousand wishes, hopeless and small
It is filled with ugliness and envy
With twilight and with weariness.
The drab everyday is full of anxiety
It is like cold cigarette smoke
So empty, stale and dull withal.
But full of memories it is too.

Everyday

Everyday is drab and gray.
No tears, no laughter,
No thoughts of thereafter
Just eat and drink and work and play
Boredom and sleep is everyday

Everyday is the day God made the world
The bottomless sea, the endless sky
The fertile plain, the mountains high
The dark abyss, death and decay
For terrible and wonderful is everyday

Everyday is the day God died for our sins
It is the day of murder, lust and war
It is the day of triumph and remorse
It is the day for you to say
Oh God, I love you every day.

  Everyday is sad and gay
It is heaven, it is the hell
It is the pearl, it is the shell
It is the start, it is the way
It's what you're making of everyday.

(Translation of a poem written in Israel)

Little Spring Song

I am longing for a little love
It is spring and I am alone
The birds sing joyous songs of love
And all young people go in pairs

Here I am walking in the park
On every bench sit two and kiss
I am ashamed I am alone
And slink away with low held head.

The night falls silently and mild
Alone I lie in bed and shiver
It feels so hot, it feels so damp
I am alone because I want

At last I fall asleep
A quiet wind blows softly
Now it is good, now I am dreaming
Now I am not alone in spring

The harsh alarm cuts through my dream
The clammy morning calls
I leave my bed and wash and dress
And greet the sober day.

I'm stepping out into the spring
The bursting buds, the blooming trees
I am alone, and wish so deep
A little love, a little love.

(Translation of a poem written in 1929 in Vienna)

Author With a German Accent

Dear brother, in reply to your masterpiece
I wish to point out to you facts like these
I am no longer able to write German rhymes
Because I think only of dollars and dimes
I hope however to achieve fame in the end
As an American author with a German accent.

(Poem written in answer to one of my brother Floh's famous poems)

English Without Fear

I accept the challenge, sister dear
Will rhyme in English without fear
And though we live "in Middle East"
Are we not world citizens at least?
In English phrases, like genteel,
We can express all that we feel
Alas, no more German to bother
Let's in future address one another
As people of the world will fit
In modern basic English writ.

(Floh's answer to "Author with a German Accent")

Stephanie in her dorm room at the agricultural school in Affuleh. Note the guitar, which she played with gusto, hanging on the wall behind her.

My First Year in Eretz Israel

My book *A Jewish Girl in the Weimar Republic* ends on my first day in Erez Israel in 1934, when it was still Palestine. During the last years of growing antisemitism in Germany, I had become a Zionist. I decided to be part of the Hechaluz, the pioneers who intended to build a society of workers and farmers, living in communes like kibbuzim and moshavim in the land of ancient Israel.

After I had to leave the university, I took a course in cooking and home making, and then worked for about a year as secretary of the Keren Kayemeth and Keren Hayessoth (the Jewish National Funds), and the local Zionistic Organization. After several run-ins with Gestapo and police, I realized that it was high time for me to leave Germany. The truth of this was later confirmed by a mention in a book *Geschichte der Juden in N*ürnberg (History of the Jews in Nürnberg, p. 227) that my activities for the Jewish National Fund were illegal, and that I was under police surveillance. I left Nürnberg to go to Hachsharah (the preparation for agricultural work in Palestine). In the meantime I applied for acceptance in an agricultural school in Erez Israel for which I had to pay a small tuition fee and my own passage.

At the time when I came to the British Mandate of Palestine, only 200,000 Jews were living in the country, and of them only a small number were Chaluzim.

Excerpts from my letters
Postcard from Trieste:

Here I stand in front of the S.S. Gerusalemme the ship that we will board in two hours. We are in a huge hall together with hundreds of Jews who will travel on the same ship with us. Among them are we 50 girls from Germany who intend to go to agricultural schools for girls. There seem to be two different groups of young people. One group wears hats or skullcaps and is formally dressed, the other wears casual dress, and is now forming a circle for dancing the horrah. I will now stop my writing and dance with them.

Letter from the board of the S.S. Gerusalemme

The mail will be leaving soon and most of the people on board are writing letters wherever they can find a place and hold a piece of paper on their lap.

Afterwards our group intends to visit the kosher chef who has promised us ice cream. Then I would like to visit the command bridge to learn more about the working of a ship. While the ship is in port, everybody can move freely about. We are confined in third class while we are on the high seas. Third class is spartan and very crowded with emigrants. Yet it is no emigrant ship like the ones we have seen in books and movies. I have seen no tears, everybody is full of hope and joy. The past is behind us and this interim on the ship is the final separation when we can find ourselves and gain strength for our new life. During the day and in the evening we attend lectures and study Hebrew.

Yesterday evening we were singing on deck when we heard the ship's band playing ballroom dance music. We went downstairs and began to dance the horrah in competition. Finally, the band played Jewish dances, and we danced until we were completely exhausted.

We are not yet forming permanent friendships, because we are flirting around. We are speculating about the schools to which we are going to be sent. Some of us will be sent to large schools with certain comforts, some to small pioneering schools. I wonder what I have to write in my next letter from Tel Aviv.

A postcard from Tel Aviv, April 30, 1934

Here I am, and it is all very unreal. The ship arrived in Jaffa at 6 A.M. It was 3:30 P.M. by the time we finished all the formalities. We had to disembark in small boats, where dark-skinned, wild looking Arabs in baggy trousers lifted us roughly from the ship into the boats. The short trip from ship to shore was smoother than we expected after we had seen the little boats popping in the water. The inoculations were not as bad as we had been made to believe.

My destiny has been finally decided. I will go with 7 other girls from our transport to Afuleh. I am happy because my companions seem to be very nice. We are going to leave tomorrow. Afuleh is near to Nahalal. I will be able to visit Ritsch and Jack Kohnstamm.

Letter from Meshek Poaloth Afuleh, May 2, 1934

This is my last day of leisure and I want to share with you the happiness of sweating in Erez Israel. It is bliss to live and work here. We have experienced more happy events in these last two days than many months in Germany.

We saw land on Monday morning at 5 P.M. Jaffa seemed to be very picturesque, high on a cliff. Next to it on the plain, the vast expanse of Tel Aviv. When we left the immigration building, we saw strange looking Arabs in long kaftans with large white kerchiefs, fastened with thick, black ropes, called agal. Most of them were riding or leading small donkeys. Some rode or led small wooden horsedrawn carts. The streets were narrow, bordered by dusty stone houses.

We took a bus to Tel Aviv where we saw the

first street signs and advertising in Hebrew. Trees
lined the streets and the people looked European. It
came as a shock to realize that they all were Jews.
We mostly saw workers in very simple attire. To me
they seemed beautiful, they looked sunburned, joyful
and proud.

A splendid meal awaited us at a school of the
WIZO (Women's International Zionistic Organization). Then we went to the post office, where I met
friends from Nürnberg. Each of us was assigned to a
family for the night. My hosts were a family named
Nussbaum.

Yesterday, Mayday, we took a bus to Afuleh.
The landscape is very interesting. We saw Jewish and
Arab villages, bare, desert like mountains, as well as
stunning serpentines with views of a large fertile
valley. We German girls were very excited and tried
to talk to all the passengers.

At the bus station in Afuleh a mule drawn
wooden farm wagon waited for us. We loaded our
luggage and then we walked behind the wagon the 20
minutes to our new home near the town. A simple
meal was prepared for us in the dismal wooden shack
that served as our dining hall. But the house where
we sleep is built of stone. Four of us sleep in each
room.

We had barely eaten, when we were rushed
again into the wagon. It had been fitted with wooden
boards on each side in which all members of the
meshek were driven to Kibbuz Mizpa for a celebration of Mayday. We sat on bales of hay in front of a
stage where a play in Hebrew was in progress. We
did not understand one word. This was followed by
music and singing. Fortunately, we knew some of the
songs and could participate. We met some of the
kibbuzniks who spoke yiddish, and we could kind of

communicate with them. Then we were treated to tea and cake.

The director of our school is Sarah Malkin a very interesting old lady who has written a book *Letters from the Second Alijah*, which has been translated, so you can get it and read it.

Our meshek is comparatively small. We have 400 dunam (acres), 1000 chickens, two mules, one horse, 2 cows and two calves. The bulk of the farm is a huge tree nursery.

My second letter from Afuleh

Before I go to sleep, I have to tell you how immensely happy I am. I don't recognize myself anymore. In the last few days an unsatisfied city slicker has been transformed into a suntanned cheerful person. The motto here is "en davar", it doesn't matter.

The life in the meshek is pleasant. We work from 5 to 7 A.M. Then we have a substantial breakfast and clean our rooms. We work again from 8 to 11. We take a shower and have lunch. Afterwards, we have to stay in our rooms, because it is too hot outside. A breeze usually starts around noon. It is very hot at first, but cools off later. Evenings are pleasantly warm. we resume work at 2 P.M. I have pulled weeds in the morning, and helped make hay in the afternoon.

So far, we have spent every evening on the roof of the one story house, singing and talking. Each month, we have to work one weekend and have three free weekends. We intend to go to Haifa for the first weekend. We have to leave Friday afternoon, because there are no buses running on the Shabbath.

We are still speaking German among ourselves, mixed with newly learned Hebrew words. We have not yet communicated much with the Polish girls and the sabras, the ones born in Erez Israel. When we arrived there were already one German boy and two German girls in the meshek who were glad to welcome us. In addition to the 10 German girls and the 10 girls who do not speak German, there are 3 male workers for the hard work and two teachers. We have plenty of land, but not enough water for intensive farming.

Afuleh, May 14, 1934

I hope you get this letter in time for your birthday, Mutch, for which I send my heartfelt wishes. Unfortunately, I have not yet received any mail from you.

I will describe today our new home. Our dorm is a modern stone building. Little bushes in front of it will grow into large trees. Each room has a window and a door on the opposite side and the house is built at an angle that catches every breeze. Outside the doors in a cemented, covered patio, so that we have shade during the hottest part of the day. In the background are Afuleh and the hills surrounding the Emek Jesreel.

My work is to irrigate the little trees in the nursery. We dig ditches around the rows of plants with a heavy hoe, called turiah. Then we let the water run through the channels. We have to be alert to repair all leaks in order not to lose any water. When I am not irrigating, I trim the little fruit trees.

Our rest and lunchbreak lasts 3 hours. Afterwards we work till sunset around 6:30. Sunset is much earlier than in Germany, by seven it is deep night.

Afuleh, May 19, 1934

I am enjoying this life which is so different from my former life. The work is physically very strenuous, but satisfying. I like the companionship with the other girls and the peacefulness of the surroundings.

Next week, our new teacher will arrive. Then we will have Hebrew lessons. Our rooms are simple, but pleasant. There are four beds, one wardrobe for all of us, three night tables, one larger table, and one chair. We have made it cheerful with our bedspreads, curtains and a tablecloth. But life is kind of monotonous. We have seen no newspapers or letters since our arrival.

Young boys and police officers from Afuleh visit the meshek in the evening, but we cannot yet talk with them. We have no electricity, but only kerosene lamps. One of the girls has a harmonica, and I have my guitar, and we share our books for nightly entertainment. For work, we wear shorts, but in the evenings, we wear dresses.

Afuleh, May 26, 1934

I had to stay a whole day in bed, because my face was swollen after a bite by a poisonous insect. I had to see a doctor, but it is better now. We had our first Chamsim, a dry wind from the desert that is very hot and uncomfortable.

I had to work in the kitchen during the first weekend. The only stoves we have are vicious kerosene stoves. In these Primus stoves, the kerosene is burned under pressure and comes out through a tiny hole that is clogged most of the time with soot. It has to be opened again and again with a special thin needle. It also makes a terrifying noise. I came to the kitchen a bit late and was supposed to boil 4 gallons of milk and bake 20 pancakes, but one of the stoves was out of order. Sarah, our director was in the kitchen to clean her lamp. I panicked and told her: "Please call one of the girls to help me, I cannot handle this by myself." She replied: "Don't worry, I will help you." Right away she repaired the stove that would not work for me. We fried the pancakes in no time. I was very impressed by her kindness.

Naftali, one of our workers, had to go to Haifa last Sunday, and I asked him to take me to Nahalal on his way. We got up at 5:30 next morning, but missed the train and had to go by bus. Arab and Jewish buses go through Afuleh, but they do not follow any schedule. One just waits at the highway until a bus comes along, or better, a private car stops to take a hitch-hiker. Sometimes a bus appears only after hours of waiting, and chances are that it is full and does not stop.

Naftali and I were lucky. An Arab bus stood at the station as we arrived, destination: "Haifa, via Nahalal". While the Jewish buses proceed through the valley, the Arab buses climb a mountain in breath-taking serpentines with a glorious view of the Emek of Jesreel to Nazareth, before coming to Nahalal. Nazareth is mostly inhabited by Christian Arabs, many of whom speak German, because there is a German school. We talked to an Arab lady. A world separates us from the Arabs. The men, standing around the bus station in Nazareth had handsome features, but they were dressed in dirty, sometimes torn kaftans. Anyway, we greeted them with a friendly shalom.

I had a hard time in Nahalal finding the Kohnstamms (Rita Kohnstamm is the niece of my

father's sister Hannchen.) Besides being related we
were good friends. She was my den mother, in the
Kameraden (the German Jewish hiking club) when I
was a young girl.

Nahalal is a Moshav, a Jewish agricultural
settlement in which the land is owned by the Keren
Kayemeth, the Jewish National Fund, and all products
are marketed through cooperative. But unlike in a
Kibbuz, each family has its own house and 125 acres
of land. This is as much as a family can farm without
hired help. But after the disaster in Germany, farmers
were each allowed to hire a new immigrant from
Germany, to teach him farming until he is ready to get
land in a new moshav and work on his own meshek.

I found Rita and Jack in a zrif, a wooden
barrack in the backyard of a farmer of Nahalal. The
zrif is quite attractive and clean once you are inside,
but they live very primitively and have to work incredibly hard. Nevertheless, they seem to be happy
and satisfied, especially Jack, the former lawyer who
took to farming like a duck in water.

There are 90 farmers in Nahalal. The houses
are built in a circle around the water tower. Next to
the water tower is a small wooden synagogue, where
the parents of the settlers hold their services. The
young people do not practice their religion. There is a
large stone building that serves as meeting house,
theater, movie house, concert hall, and medical center.
Also in the center is the administration building, the
only general store, the school, the agricultural cooperative, and wooden huts for the craftsmen, like tailor,
shoemaker, blacksmith, harnessmaker, etc.

Some of the farmers still live in their original
wooden shacks, but more than half of them have built
modest stone or concrete houses with 2 rooms, veranda, kitchen, and a small indoor bathroom. The old

wooden barracks had outhouses. The villagers hope that by the end of the year, every settler will have a permanent house. In front of each house is a small flower garden, and behind each house is the land that can be irrigated. Here every farmer is free to plant what he wants: vegetables, fruit trees, citrus trees, or green fodder for the animals. Near the house are the stables. Each family owns between 6 to 10 cows, a horse or a mule, and about 100 chickens.

Beyond the circle of irrigated land are the fields. Each farmer has 4 plots, one for wheat, one for corn, one for hay, and a share in the small forest. They have crop rotation, and plot rotation. All inhabitants have more or less the same standard of living. The members of the moshav think that their system is the ideal way of living without exploiting anybody, living off the land as a community, and still have the comfort of a closely knit family and property (in contrast to the kibbutz where everything is shared)

Shabbath is the day of rest. No work is done in the fields, but animal and household chores have to be done, shabbath or not.

The children go to school, even the very small ones go to nursery school. Nevertheless, the lives of the women is unbelievably hard. They have to cook, do the laundry by hand, look after the babies, milk the cows, take care of the chickens, and work in the vegetable garden.

Life in the Kibbutz is much easier, especially for women who have regular working hours. But I will write about the Kibbutz when I have had more experience.

Rita and Jack, and my friend Meir Wollner live in the shacks that have been vacated by settlers who now live in permanent houses. They wait there for land to be allocated to them by the National Fund.

Haifa, May 29, 1934

Chag Habikurim is the feast of the first har-
vest. It coincides with the feast of Shavuoth, when in
biblical times the Jews made their pilgrimage to the
temple in Jerusalem to sacrifice the first born of their
animals and the first fruit of the season. This custom
has been revived, but they bring their fruits and
animals to the Jewish National Fund in Haifa, not to
the temple.

Children reenact the sacrifice in the temple,
but they sing modern Hebrew songs. I went with
Meir and his friends to the festivities in Nahalal.
After the performance we sang and danced till midnight. I slept late the next morning. We wanted to go
to Haifa in the afternoon, but had to wait 1 1/2 hours
in the burning sun until an Arab bus stopped for us. I
got a bad sunburn. We arrived in Haifa in time to see
the parade of the first fruits. Every kibbuz, every
moshav in the area had a float, and in between were
marching children, horsemen and bands.

My heart leapt for joy as I saw those happy
Jewish farmers show off their products as lambs, kids,
corn, wheat, eggs, butter, honey, and vegetables. Each
float was decorated with the greatest love and care
with the simplest of means. Some of the floats had
political slogans, but the main theme of the parade
was the love of the land and the farming of the earth.
The children were mostly sabras, children born in
Erez Israel.

The parade ended at the Technion, the techni-
cal university of Haifa, where Menachem Ussishkin
accepted the gifts in the name of the Keren Kayemeth.

We had supper with Meir's sister, and though
dead tired, went to a performance in the amphitheater.
Actors of the Habimah, the national theater, assisted

by amateurs reenacted the pilgrimage to Jerusalem and afterwards the story of Ruth.

I was able to find a bus to Afuleh. I instantly fell asleep and nearly missed getting out at my destination. At 1:30 A.M. I stood shivering at the station, afraid to walk alone in the darkness. But I took heart and started walking, when a policeman stopped me. "You can not walk alone in the night." He took me to the police station and phoned the meshek that somebody had to come to pick me up. However, the watchman told him that he could not leave his post, and everybody else was sleeping. So I had to walk home with a police escort.

That was Monday. Tuesday was the only working day of that week. Wednesday was a boycott against the British government, because of a reduction in the immigration certificates for Jews. We went to a rally in the synagogue, but I could not understand the speeches.

I could not work Friday and Saturday, because my face was again swollen from insect bites. My face itched intolerably, and I had to put compresses on it all day long Saturday I rode our old sweet mare Shushanka for the first time.

My pretty roommate Leah Hirsch flirted on the ship with a rich Zionist leader, David Ullman from Karlsbad, who fell in love with her. He came to the meshek to visit her and to invite her to a tour of the country. She told him: "I would love to, but I cannot go without a chaperon." She asked me to come along. I was quite excited, but we were afraid to ask Sarah to let us go. To our surprise, David had already buttered up our boss. She gave us her blessings.

David had a room rented for us in Haifa at a fancy hotel with an unforgettable view of the city and the bay. It was full moon, and the beauty of the night made me tremble. A gourmet meal was served on the balcony: Paté de foi gras, fresh lox, gourmet cheeses and coffee. It felt strange after the privations of our present life.

After a wonderful breakfast, we went the next morning to the spectacular park of the Bahai temple. Then we bought fruits, chocolate and candies for our trip.

David had rented a car with a chauffeur and we drove without stopping to Tiberias. The way led through Arab lands where the peasants cut the wheat in the fields with old-fashioned sickles. We saw the threshing of the wheat in the villages as it is described in the Bible. The wheat is piled up on wooden sleds with young boys on them and driven round and round over the wheat. Finally, the men throw the wheat with their pitchforks high into the air. The lighter straw is carried away by the wind, while the heavier grains fall back to earth. So the wheat is separated from the chaff.

In contrast, we saw tractors and combines where the grains fall into sacks, and the straw comes out in neatly packed bundles in the fields of the Jewish settlement through which we traveled.

We finally glimpsed the deep blue of Lake Tiberias below in a valley. We descended in sweeping serpentines, the lake at 300 feet below sea level.

We had soft drinks and walked through the city which is inhabited by 5,000 Jews and 2,000 Arabs. We saw ruins of Herod's palace and walked through the colorful bazaar. After a delightful meal of fresh fish from the lake we continued south to Daganiah, the oldest Kwuza (Kwuzah is a small kibbuz). We got a tour of the kwuzah, and met some people we knew, but our stay was short. We continued to drive south to the great electrical generator, and reservoir, the Ruthenberg Works. It is hot like in a cauldron, and we gladly turned north again.

From a vantage point, we saw the Transjordanian police, reminding us how small the country really is. We swam in the lake and had tea on the terrace of an elegant hotel. Then we drove up the mountains of Galilee to the northern border with Lebanon in Metullah. We passed through the Hule region with its swamps. The Arabs who live in this region are all infected with malaria. They live in reed huts, much like Babylonians lived thousands of years ago. We read in our guide book that you can find wild boars and buffaloes in this area. While we read this, we actually saw a herd of buffalo.

It was cold and dark, when we arrived in Metullah. We had to show our passports to the frontier police. We slept well in the brisk mountain air. The breakfast was a full meal with tomatoes, cucumbers, eggs, three kinds of cheese, butter, jam, and coffee. After breakfast we went to see the famous waterfall. It was a dangerous steep descent through fields that were covered with thistles and wild flowers. Then we came to a valley of a narrow brook where a large herd of cattle and horses was led to drink. The canyon got narrow and narrower. We walked through a gorge with steep rocks on both sides. The gorge ends, and from the tops of the cliffs tumbles a silvery water fall. We sat on a ledge, and silently admired the beauty and tranquillity of the scene.

From Metullah we drove south to Kfar Gileadi with a monument in honor of Trumpeldor, the defender of the Galil against the Arabs. We passed next to Lake Huleh again, but did not see any more buffaloes. Then we continue to Rosh Pinah which contains the custom house of the Syrian frontier. We climbed to the upper Galilee on a scenic road to Safed, which lies on top of a mountain. We visited the old synagogue where we were told that there was a community of talmud scholars throughout the ages, when the Jews were dispersed throughout the world and had no homeland.

We drank, for me it was the first time, the strong sweet Turkish coffee. Our next stop was in Meron which also was a center of talmudic learning. The mountainside was very rocky, and all the vegetation we saw was brown and dry grass and thistles. Once the rocks are removed, this land may become fruitful again as it was in biblical times, if we have enough purpose, money and water for this task.

Our guide in Meron was an old Jew, dressed in a silk kaftan like Arabs are wearing. He could speak Hebrew, Arabic, French, Yiddish and English. We entered the synagogue and lit candles in memory of Rabbi Hillel. We saw another ancient synagogue and the tombs of Hillel, Shammai and the 36 Zaddikim. As we stumbled through the rocky fields, we had the strange sensation of being in a place that had much historic significance.

On our way back to Haifa, we drove again through Arab land and through an agricultural experimental station of the British government. The herds we saw grazing on the hills were a mixture of black goats and funny looking Palestinian sheep that have heavy, fat tails hanging behind them. Some villages were inhabited by Jews who lived there through centuries and looked the same as the Arabs.

Then we came to Acre which is inhabited by Arabs. We walked though the shuk, or market, which was dirty, and did not smell very nice, but was colorful and noisy. In the open coffee houses sat Arabs on low stools, smoking waterpipes, also called narguilehs or hubble bubbles. We were soon surrounded by a group of youngsters who were begging aggressively for a backsheesh, a gift of money. We saw the beautiful mosque and the huge imposing prison from the outside. We climbed on top of the fortifications from the Crusader's time, that even Napoleon could not conquer. The walls drop steeply down to the sea, where the waves break against them with white tufts of foam.

We returned to the car through narrow lanes, and drove around the bay back to Haifa. To our right were the yellow dunes and the blue sea. To our left were mostly swamps that may become settlements one day. We passed through Kiriath Chaim, named after Chaim Arlossoroff. It is a clean oasis in the midst of sand with little stone houses and gardens and flowers. The reason for this miracle is sweet water. Water can transform the most desolate desert into life and make plants grow like magic.

Back in Haifa, Leah and I sat on the balcony writing like mad. Then we were called for a lovely dinner. Afterwards we had a walk with David Ullman through Hadar Hacarmel, the center of Jewish Haifa.

This morning we are busy again with our epistles. I have to tell you more about Haifa. It is built on the slopes of Mount Carmel which is covered by forests, and reaches down to the deep blue Mediterranean. The Arab town near the seashore is hustle and bustle, and full of dust. But as soon as you go up to Hadar Hacarmel, you are in a modern city with attractive houses that are separated from each other by small gardens. Each house has balconies or verandas. Herzl Street has many small coffee houses and shops full of people, a real metropolitan street. But above and below it are quiet villas and apartment houses. They are modern with all comforts. The floors of the apartments are of ceramic tiles, and each flat has a modern bathroom. Between the houses are still many more houses in construction, and empty lots. Each week, new houses are completed.

In my next letter, you will probably hear about more adventures. We are not going back to the meshek, but on to Tel Aviv.

Leah's friend, David Ulman seems to be quite influential. He promised to contact you in Germany when he comes back, and will try to help you with your emigration.

I hope that my brother Floh will be able to come in fall. His chances of finding work as a carpenter are quite good. Many idealistic young people who start work in agriculture have to give up. They have to support their parents, and the new settlements are still too poor to accept and support old people. Many of them now work in construction where the wages are quite high. The temptation to quit farming is great. Sometimes it is to support a family, sometimes it is greed. The Hechaluz is still intent to get as many immigrants as possible into agriculture, which is the backbone of Zionism.

Please give my letter to my friends and family, because I cannot write to all of them.

Givath Brenner, June 5, 1934

I have another week of new experiences that I want to share with you. Tomorrow we will go back to work and studies.

After lunch, we went to Khayat beach, the nicest beach around Haifa, to swim. Then we drove to the top of Mount Carmel. There is a small Jewish colony of villas, and several convents, hospitals, and hotels. We had ice cream, and then David Ullman, Leah's friend, took us to the railway station and we said goodbye.

It was 10:30 P.M. when we arrived in Tel Aviv.

Leah told me that I could sleep with her in the house of her relatives. But she had forgotten their address, and only vaguely remembered their house. It took us more than one hour to find it. They fed us and gave us one narrow bed to sleep on, where we slept more or less. (more less than more) But the next morning we were rewarded by a swim in the sea. For the next night, I got an invitation to sleep at the home of Liesel Alexander, a former schoolmate from Nürnberg.

During the afternoon, we went to the "Taruchah", the Levant Fair. We were both impressed, especially with the hall, "Tozereth Haarez" in which products by the Jews of Erez Israel are exhibited. The "Histadruth", the Jewish Labor Union also had an impressive exhibit. There was an interesting pavilion by the British government. The exhibits by the other 36 participating countries were repetitive and exhausting. They were of articles that are at present imported, or could be imported. We had trouble understanding the captions of the exhibits, because we were proficient in none of the official languages: Hebrew, English, and Arabic. Anyway, tired as we were, we were glad to see this impressive testimony to Jewish revival in Erez Israel.

The next morning, we took the bus to Rechovoth, where we visited my former school friend Hanni Nussbaum in Kibbuz Givath Brenner. She has lived there for a long time.

(What I did not write in my letter, was that I had a severe asthma attack in Givath Brenner, and they could not find a doctor during Shabbath. I fought desperately for air for more than 48 hour without sleep. When I finally got an injection, I was so weak that I could not get up for another day. It was one of the worst experience of my life.)

The Kibbuz Givath Brenner is beautiful. In Germany, we pictured the life in a Kibbuz as a life of

privations that we could only endure because it was
our duty to build up our land. That was the philoso-
phy of the "Second Alijah" the pioneers at the turn of
the century who founded Daganiah and other
Kibbuzim in the Galilee. Actually, it is a happy life
for a working person. Labor is well distributed and
each worker has enough free time. Of course, at the
beginning, life is very simple. Newcomers live in old
army tents, and the food is extremely simple. As soon
as the economy of the group improves, zrifs and
houses are built, and life becomes more comfortable.

Hanni and her husband have a tent, about 12
feet in diameter. It is high and well ventilated. The
floor is made of ceramic tiles. They have a bed, a
table, two low stools, a small cupboard, made of
empty crates, but they also have flowers, a nice
bedcover, a tablecloth, a kerosene lamp, a ceramic
bowl with fruits and a little cot on which I slept.
Hanni's husband is tall and handsome, and her baby is
adorable.

The baby lives in the "Beth Hajeladim", the
children's house. Hanni spends enough time with the
baby because she is nursing him. The parents spend
much of their free time with their children and put
them to bed in the evening. People work usually 8
hours a day, and sometimes even less in winter.

The food in Givath Brenner is nutritious and
abundant. They eat meat twice a week, but many
vegetables, salads and dairy products. Everybody
eats in the "Chadar Ochel", the communal dining hall.
It is attractive with wood paneling, curtains, and
oilcloth on the tables. The Kibbuz has also a library, a
record player with many classic records, newspaper,
and scheduled Hebrew courses. Right now the popu-
lation consists of 300, mostly young people, and 50
children. Each group of tents has a shower house.
There is electricity in the main buildings, but not in

the living quarters.

Each person has a compartment in the "Machsan" (machsan is a warehouse, but is used for the wardrobe building and laundry). Members deposit their dirty and torn laundry in a basket, and find it clean and mended in their compartment at the end of the week. It is really a carefree life, especially for the women, who do not have the chores of a household. The daily cleaning of the tent does not take more than ten minutes, and the hours after the assigned work are leisure. Fifty percent of the Chawerim (members) are German and still speak too much German.

Rare photo of Stephanie on horseback at the Ag school.

Healthy, tanned and trim Stephanie standing in the field at Affulleh.

The house on Sekilaridis Street.

Jacob and Stephanie Orfali, the newlyweds in their first apartment, before moving into the Sekilaridis hause.

The Sekilaridis House

Last week I walked into a classroom in Waukegan, Illinois as a substitute teacher. On the wall was a calendar with a picture of Jerusalem. In the picture I found the Sekilaridis house, which I first saw on a sunny April morning in 1941, thirty years ago.

I consider the seven years we lived in this house as the happiest years of my life. I said to my mother several times, "I will never again complain in my life, because I have experienced as much happiness in the Sekilaridis House as anyone could ask for in a lifetime".

As I look back and remember "the seven happy years", it seems strange that we were so deliriously happy. Those seven years were as full of strife, sickness and heartbreak as some of the most unhappy years of our life.

How we found the house

Jacob and I were living with George, our oldest boy who was six months old, in a one room apartment with a tiny kitchen in the modern part of Jerusalem. We decided it was time to look for roomier quarters. To look for an apartment was one of our favorite pastimes but the housing shortage was acute because when thousands of Jewish immigrants from Germany settled in Palestine like a swarm of locusts. Rents soared skywards and we had bad experiences with sharing an apartment.

Jacob asked his friends at work whether they knew of a place for rent. One morning he told me to look at the Sekilaridis house on Amireh Road, right next to the cemetery and one block west of the Jewish Agency. I put George in his baby carriage and went to find the house. I did not enter the house. It sat near the top of a hill and was build of solid limestone with gaily painted blue window shutters and a red tile roof. The most striking feature was a second floor balcony that ran the whole width of the house, facing east. The wrought iron fence of the balcony was filled with a chain of blooming flowers in big pots. Sofas and chairs lined the wall, like seats on a balcony of a theater. An old Arab cemetery was in the foreground and the old city of Jerusalem and the Mount of Olive as a backdrop. Just like the stage of a grand opera. I saw only the balcony that occupied the whole west front of the house. A balcony full of flower pots bursting with carnations and geraniums. Through the gate, I also saw a patio ringed by flower pots and a ramshackle house. When Jacob came home, I told him I didn't care how the house looked inside, I wanted to rent it at any cost.

We were not of sound mind at the time

The inside of the house was something else. It was absolutely impossible, but I had made up my mind. First of all, we saw tell tale signs of bed bugs in most of the rooms, second it did not have running water. The only water supply was in the beautiful Patio which had a cistern from which we had to pump all our water and then carry it upstairs. Jacob filled a large earthenware jar with water every morning before he went to work. If I needed more, I had to pump and carry it myself. The house had an indoor toilet, of course, but without flushing facilities and no bath. The house had six rooms. The two front rooms had linoleum floors, the other four rooms had rough wooden boards as floors. There was a narrow and long hall at the end of which was a small windowless room that would be our kitchen. The kitchen was a dark hole without any plumbing. A four gallon kerosine canister with a spigot at the bottom was the running water, which was filled by Jacob every morning. A big bowl under the canister was the kitchen sink. Kitchen utensils, pots and pans stood on shelves around the walls. Instead of an oven, I had two kerosine stoves, one a primus stove that had a hot flame and another with a wick that cooked slowly and kept food warm. Both stoves created a layer of soot under the cooking pots which had to be scrubbed daily.

We needed only the two front rooms, the hall and the kitchen for our own use, so we decided to sublet the other four rooms for needed income. The catch was that the toilet was in the back of the house. We would have to go through one of the rooms we needed to rent in order to go to the toilet and to throw away the water we had used. The toilet was the only place in the house which was connected to the sewer and every drop of water used in the house had to find its outlet through the toilet bowl. The shower was a four gallon kerosine canister that had a shower head on its bottom and could be lifted and lowered by a cable that ran through a pulley. We lowered the container, filled it with water, lifted it and secured the cable. To take a shower we stood in a large round basin and emptied the water in the toilet afterward.

Nobody in his sound mind would have rented the place. It seems that we were not of a sound mind at that time, because Jacob agreed with me that regardless of the insane arrangement, this would be the house for us.

It was very easy to rent the four rooms to student nurses in the nearby baby home. We even found a girl for the room through which we had to pass. She was poor, and really happy to live for so little rent. As an added advantage, she would baby sit for George at least once a week. This was important for us because we were movie fans and had large families to go visit.

The bedbugs were another story. We contained them, but we never got completely rid of them. They could hide in the nooks and crannies of the old house, and as soon as we had finished off one generation, the eggs would hatch, and the game of extermination would start anew. But everything has its bright side. Because of my eternal war against the bugs, our house was kept spotlessly clean. Our furniture, which I had brought with me from Germany, looked great in the large, high living room. We bought a cheap dresser and a crib for George's room. The balcony had morning sun, which was great for hanging the washing. It was in the shade during the afternoon, which was great for sitting outside, enjoying the incredible view, and drinking coffee. Except for rainy days in winter, the balcony became our living room, and the cistern place became our dance floor for our numerous parties.

Jacob worked for the Soconny Vacuum Oil Company of New Jersey at that time. First he worked in the office which was just a few blocks away, down the mountain. Later he was a traveling auditor, a job that took him to all parts of the country. I had a part time job as secretary of the Society for the Hard of Hearing. The office was in our house. My office hours were from two to five every afternoon, but I had few clients. Part of my job was to collect the pledged contributions for the School for the Deaf. When I went on my collection tour I always had a baby in a carriage or stroller along.

Tante Hede

A few weeks after we moved into our new house, I met my poor maiden aunt, Tante Hede, while I was shopping near our house. Tante Hede was dying slowly from cancer. We all knew it, but we weren't sure whether she was aware of it. Tante Hede was such a brave lonely soul. She was a door to door saleslady of cosmetics and household articles, like a Fuller Brush salesperson. She was happy that she could get along again after her severe operation and would not have missed the visits to her clients for anything. Most of her clients were very nice to her, and often treated her to a cup of coffee. Coffee was her only vice. She would drink it with gusto at any time of day or night. So, of course, I invited her home for a cup of coffee. But before we went home, she proudly bought a sun bonnet for little George because she thought that the sun was shining in his eyes and disturbing him. I showed her around our house and she rested her tired feet while I made a good and strong cup of coffee for her. she said "Coffee is the greatest joy in my life. I hope somebody will make me a good cup of coffee before I die."

This was the last time I saw her alive. Two days later she came home exhausted after a hot morning of walking and selling. Her landlady gave her dinner and later a cup of coffee. Then she heard a funny noise from Tante Hede's room. Tante Hede lay dead on the floor. The cup was empty. She had died without pain and after drinking her beloved coffee. It was the most peaceful death I ever have seen. When I came to the house she was still lying on the floor with the most happy and contented expression on her waxen face. The little bonnet she bought for George was worn by all my children until it finally fell to pieces.

Conversion to Catholicism

1941 was the time of the Nazi advance through North Africa. We were all afraid that the Germans would conquer Jerusalem soon and destroy all the Jews as they were doing in Europe. Jacob was frantic with fear. We Jews took it much more calmly.

Jacob and I were married by a Catholic priest in a civil ceremony. In a country where all the marriages were conducted by either a rabbi, a priest or a Moslem Cleric, mixed marriages were discouraged and nearly unheard of. We had to get a special permit from the Patriarch of Jerusalem and I had to give a solemn promise to raise all our children as Catholics. Still, the parish priest was unwilling to marry us because he had bad experiences with mixed marriages. He said that most Jewish girls who marry Catholics leave their husbands sooner or late to rejoin their Jewish community. The poor Catholic husband is married for life and cannot remarry because there is no divorce in the Catholic Church. Jacob's parents had gone to the priest and begged him not to marry us. But the Patriarch had told the priest to perform the ceremony and he had to marry us.

When George was born, he was baptized in the Armenian Catholic Church in a very impressive ceremony. The Armenians baptize their babies by immersion. Little George was lovely and quiet while he got his bath in the fount. Afterwards we went to my parents in law who had finally accepted me and were proud of their first grandson. My mother also went to the baptism and reception. The happiest person at the baptism was Mairik, Jacob's old nurse, who adopted our children as if they were her own grandchildren.

While we were celebrating in one room, I stole out to look at the sleeping baby. George looked radiantly peaceful, still glowing with the holy oil with which he had been anointed. I had a strange feeling of remoteness. This child who was part of me, who was so incredibly near to me since his birth four weeks ago, lived suddenly in a Religious world of his own which was closed to me.

So, when Jacob urged me to become Catholic I was not adamant in my refusal, as I had been before. I knew, contrary to Jacob's belief, that a conversion to Catholicism would not save me from Hitler's wrath, should he ever conquer Jerusalem. However, I agreed to take instruction in the Christian faith in order to please

Jacob.

For the next 6 weeks I went dutifully twice a week to the Reparatrice Nuns, a strict contemplative religious order. A sweet old nun who spoke French and English (I think she was Canadian) was my teacher. I burdened her with all my doubts, but obediently read the New Testament and the history of the Catholic Church and the numerous lives of the Saints. Jacob supplemented the instructions by taking me to all the places in and around Jerusalem that are mentioned in the New Testament. Jacob, unfortunately, has missed his calling. He should never have worked in an office. He was born to be a tourist guide. His happiest pastime was and still is to show his beloved Jerusalem to anybody who is willing to be guided by him. A great deal of my love for Jerusalem is due to his expert guidance. The gospel stories became alive while we visited churches, ruins and the villages around Jerusalem. I could see Jesus and his disciples as if they were still present, and the stories of the gospel became more real.

Looking back, I don't know whether I really believed, or whether I wanted to believe. When the good nun finally gave me the words of the baptismal ceremony, I read the text: "What do you want from the Catholic Church?" and my answer "The Faith." I convinced myself that I could get the real faith only after baptism, and that my doubts would vanish after I received the Sacrament. I don't know whether it was self deception or faith that let me consent to be baptized, because in the depth of my being I knew that whatever happens I would always remain a Jew.

Jacob was very happy that I finally shared his religion. My mother in law was my godmother. The only sensation I felt during the ceremony was that the oil was rancid and had a bad smell. But I was happy, since everybody else was so happy.

I went faithfully to Mass and benediction not only on Sundays, but as often as I could manage. I did not have to go to confession before the baptism, because the sacrament of baptism would by itself cleanse me of all my previous sins. I was supposed to be as innocent as a newborn baby.

So far, so good. The dilemma began when I went to the

Patriarch for my first confession. I do not remember whether he asked, or whether I volunteered the information, but I admitted that I used artificial means of birth control. The Patriarch became very serious and explained that this was a mortal sin. He could not give me absolution unless I would stop that heinous practice. I was heartbroken. I would not be able to take Holy Communion on Christmas, my whole conversion was a farce. How could Jacob claim to be a good Catholic and be an advocate of birth control?

We did not resolve the question of birth control at that time but found a temporary reprieve which emerged nine months later as a lovely baby girl, our beloved Gabrielle.

Mairik, the loving washer woman

It was not easy to keep house, clean, and cook when you have to pump every drop of water, and carry it upstairs and then carry it through a rented room to the back of the house to pour it into the toilet, especially when you are pregnant. I needed some help. Mairik was happy to come once a week to do our washing. Mairik was a widow who lived in a tiny room in the Armenian compound. She was a beautiful young woman back in Armenia before World War I. This was the time of the massacres. Her husband was killed in front of her eyes and she ran into a river with her three children. The Turkish soldiers who had killed her husband stood waiting at the edge of the river. She was afraid they would rape her in front of the children when she came out. In her despair she drowned her children by holding their heads under water and then she lost consciousness. She was found all blackened and with distended belly several miles downstream by friendly people who nursed her back to health and finally sent her to Jerusalem.

Since then she led a lonely life of working, fasting and prayer to atone for the sin of killing her children. Mairik could neither read nor write. All she knew how to do was to clean and wash and to love. She was a wisp of a woman. Her frail, emaciated body was shrouded in black rags, her eyes were watery and dim from the many tears she had shed in her life. Her face was lined with deep wrinkles, yet she was capable of a radiant smile. She had adopted Jacob as her own when she worked in his parents house, and now she extended her love to me and our children. When she arrived in the morning for a day's work, she showered us with kisses and embraces. I know that she prayed for us every single day. She enjoyed good food, and I always cooked something I knew she would like. I made her coffee strong and sweet, because she, like Tante Hede, was a coffee addict. But Mairik fasted very Wednesday and Friday, and all the forty days of lent when she would eat neither meat nor fish, nor milk or cheese only bread, fruits and vegetables.

I used to pay Mairik fair wages, but she gave most of her money to the Church for the poor. She kept just enough to stay her barely alive. All the time she was not working, she spent in prayer, met her frequently in the Church of the Holy Sepulcher. This gave her great pleasure, as she was very concerned about my salvation.

We had a little shed in our yard, and it was there that Mairik did the washing. Jacob pumped several 4 gallon canisters full of water before he went to work on a wash day and I lit the big primus stove before Mairik's arrival. She went to work right away after the kissing and embracing. She would not eat breakfast before the bed sheets were washed and boiling of the primus stove. She washed with her bare hands, without a washboard, crouched on her haunches on the floor steadily, until her hands were all white and swollen. Then she asked for a little salt. When she rubbed her hands with the salt, water would be drawn out of her hands.

Around noon, when it was warm enough, I would take the baby George down to her shed and she would bathe him lovingly and thoroughly. The baby cried pitifully, but bathing a baby was her greatest joy of which I could not deprive her. I could not speak to Mairik, because my Armenian was limited to a few polite phrases and a small number of words connected with the washing. When Jacob came home for dinner, words would pour out of her like water from a river that had been dammed up and was at last released. Jacob had no time to translate her torrent of conversation. To this day, I do not know what it was she had so urgently to tell someone.

Mairik rests now after her hard life. She was blind at the end

Her neighbors took care of her until she died. I visited her shortly before her death. She was overjoyed to see me again and so was I as I embraced the poor tiny hunchbacked skeleton that contained only love and no bitterness.

Our first four years in the Sekilaridis house were the years of World War II. For us, of the British Mandate of Palestine, they were relatively peaceful years. The terrorism between Jews and Arabs, as well as Jews or Arabs against the British administration were temporarily suspended. Many of our young people fought with the British army in Italy and Egypt. British soldiers, stationed in Palestine, or just recuperating here were fairly well treated because the Jews were united with them in their battle against the Nazis of Germany. At that time we did not yet know the full truth about the extermination camps. We feared and trembled for our dear ones that we left behind in Europe, but we heard little from them. We had a Red Cross message from my brother in Denmark, and just hoped that he was still alive after the takeover of Denmark by the Germans.

Gabrielle is born

While I was pregnant with Gabrielle I felt very well and happy. Only toward the last month, end of August 1942, I had a small mishap while hanging the washing. I lost a considerable amount of water. Alarmed, I went to the doctor at the French Hospital in Bethlehem, where I intended to give birth. He reassured me that it was nothing serious. However, I should rest as much as possible during the last month and not hang any more washing.

September passed quickly and in pleasant routine, except that fighting broke out in Syria and Lebanon. My labor pains started on the 28th of September, the day I expected them, exactly 9 months after our ribald New Years celebration. Jacob went with me by bus to Bethlehem and returned to work. The midwife reassured him that everything was fine, but it would probably take the whole day. I spent a peaceful day reading and walking in the pleasant gardens of the hospital. Jacob called at noon, and later in the evening. We had no news for him and everything was under control, so he went home and waited for the next morning. Around eight in the evening the pains finally got very strong but the midwife could not notice any progress. I told her to call the doctor. She just shrugged her shoulders. "The doctor is not here, he has joined the Free French Army. He is now in Lebanon." "Then call a doctor from Jerusalem", I said. "That's against our policy and with the blackout, the road to Jerusalem is closed, nobody can come from Jerusalem."

I got panicky. The pains grew unbearable, and no progress seemed to show. She said that the reason for the slow progress was that I had lost all the water. She could not do a thing about it, but she became very nervous herself and did not inspire any confidence. A healthy looking 9 pound girl was born around midnight. We never know whether Gabrielle's birthday was on the 28th or 29th, because the midwife was too busy to look at the watch. I lay trembling awake the whole night after the ordeal, too miserable to enjoy that it was all over.

I was baldly torn up, but there was nobody to repair the damage. I just had to keep my fingers crossed that there would not be an infection. I nursed the baby the next morning, Jacob, my mother, my mother in law and little George came to visit me and I finally calmed down and rested. On the fifth day my baby began to loose more and more weight and started to turn yellow as a lemon. I was much too weak to get up. A pediatrician from Bethlehem whom we called in just shook his head and prescribed a medicine that did not help, but started diarrhea around the clock.

On the seventh day, I could not stand it any more. I took my poor yellow baby and went home. When we weighed the baby at home there were only 5 pounds left of our 9 pounder. The poor baby lost blood every hour or more often. I spent the whole day changing diapers. It seemed hopeless.

Our doctor, a distant cousin of my mother, Dr. Sigismund Cohn from Berlin, left his practice and devoted all his time to us. This was shortly after the discovery of Penicillin, but no Penicillin was available in Palestine and we had run out of sulfa drugs because of the war. Dr. Sigismund called every doctor in town, every pharmacy, but to no avail. He consulted with a famous pediatrician, but she told him, "you are wasting your time. This is a hopeless case." Finally, 3 tablets of a sulfa drug got found in the baby home. These tablets saved Gabrielle's life. It took another week of 24 hour care t bring her out of danger.

I felt strong abdominal pains by that time, but had no time to think about it. When the baby was two weeks old, I could not get up. I had pains. The pains were worse than childbirth. I could not move, and ran a very high fever. Jacob had to call Dr. Cohn who diagnosed appendicitis in a stage were they could not get me to a hospital.

The search for a few sulfa tablets began anew. I don't remember more than a haze of pain and fear of death as I lay motionless without eating or drinking, but fully aware of the situation. The baby was sent to the baby home, George was sent to Jacob's mother. My breasts were full of milk and added to my discomfort. Finally sulfa tablets were found, gradually the fever abated, the danger was past.

I even nursed the baby again after I felt better because at that time we could not find a suitable substitute for mother's milk for our delicate daughter. We had to nurse Gabrielle through a severe bronchitis before she finally recovered. I had to postpone my own operation until the baby was clearly out of danger. I lived through the next five months with constant pain. Poor doctor Cohn carefully weighed the chances of survival for me and the baby.

The pain stopped the day of my operation. The funny thing was how much better I felt right after the operation and during my convalescence than I had felt for the preceding five months.

When Gabrielle was a year old we took a photo of her and sent a copy to our beloved doctor. "Without you, we could have never taken this picture" we wrote on it.

We had a hard time raising Gabrielle. She nearly died when she had the measles, and even chicken pox were a disaster for her. But she was the sweetest, happiest, loveliest child to recompense us for all the trouble we had with her.

Raising Pigs

Many of our Christian friends made money during the war years by raising pigs. In those lean years, pork was welcome and well paid. We had a suitable basement and backyard, to accommodate a few pigs, but in the house next to ours was a Talmud-Thora School and the rabbis would have strongly objected to pigs under their nose in the Holy City of Jerusalem.

Then we had a lucky break. The house of the Talmud Thora School was requisitioned as billets by the Military Police of the British Army in order to create a buffer zone between the warring Arabs and Jews. Jacob was able to convince the British Commander that we were neutral and our house became one of two civilian houses in the military enclave.

On a Sunday afternoon, soon after, we visited Jacob's Aunt, Soeur Justine, a nun in the French Convent of St. Joseph in Bethlehem. Soeur Justine showed us the school, the gardens, the poultry yard, the pigsty, the wine cellar and regaled us with wine, cookies and candies. Jacob and I were deeply impressed by the immense, rosy and fat pigs.

"After all the Jews have moved out, nobody would object if we had pigs," said Jacob.

"The soldiers might even sell us their swill," I piped in.

We returned home that evening with bouquets of flowers, as well as fruits from the convent garden, and forgot all about the pigs.

On the Saturday, following our visit, a shiny black limousine with a liveried chauffeur drew up to the gate of the military compound. The officer on duty stopped the car. To his surprise he saw a nun in the back seat with three tiny, rosy pigs playing around her black skirt. After he had recovered from his shock, he directed the limousine to our house.

Soeur Justine proudly presented us with the cute little creatures. We installed them in our empty basement room. We offered her and the chauffeur coffee and cake and also invited the sergeant major of the sergeant's mess. We explained to him our situation and he agreed to sell us the leftovers of their mess for a nominal sum.

Every morning, before going to work, Jacob picked up the pail with the swill. At the beginning it was much more than our tiny rosy animals could eat. However they grew at an astonishing rate and everyday they ate more. Nevertheless, even in their new dimensions, they remained affectionate and clean. They used only one corner of their abode as a bathroom, and by rolling in the dry dust in the yard, they kept themselves clean. George and Gaby loved to play with them. They roamed most of the day freely in our yard. From

time to time, we forgot to close the gate. They got out and prom-
enaded all over the military compound, even up to the King George
Avenue. The military police knew them, arrested them and always
brought them home.

When I looked at the rosy beasts, I dreamed of lovely pink
bedsheets and pillowcases. In the meantime we developed a wonderful friendship with the British soldiers. We were invited to their pub.
Often a dozen eggs or a side of bacon found its way into the swill
pail. On the other hand, the soldiers liked to sit on our veranda in the
afternoon to drink a cup of coffee and eat a piece of homemade cake.

By Christmas, our pigs were fully grown and became pork.
We sold two of them and had one of them slaughtered for a feast in
our backyard. I do not remember how many guests ate roast pork
and German potato salad and drank convent wine that Christmas Eve
in our house, but it seemed like the whole British army.

Our satisfying social life

Our social life was deeply satisfying. We had many friend in
the Jewish community. My parents lived nearby. They operated a
wholesale business of cosmetics and household articles, which
supplied mostly door to door salespeople, like Tante Hede and other
elderly refugees from Germany who eked out a marginal existence.
My brother Heinz tried to supply beauty shops and barber shops with
his articles. He had many customers among the Arabs in the old city.
My mother, who had led such a sheltered life in Germany with
servants and a large comfortable house, took readily to her new life
as a shop keeper. She patiently listened to the tales of woe of her
peddler clients, and got very troubled excited because she could
never balance the accounts.

While her sister Hede was addicted to coffee, my mother was
addicted to pastry and sweets. So am I, her equally overweight
daughter. We indulged in our vices as often as we could. As soon as
I was done with my household chores, even on days when Mairik sat
down in the yard slaving away, I dressed the children, pushed the
baby carriage up the hill to King George Avenue and to Mama's
store. Mama hungrily expected me. Whenever she could find
somebody to keep the store open she would come with me and the

children, first just George, later George and Gabrielle and just before
our seven happy years came to an end, George, Gabrielle and Joseph

Jerusalem was, and still is, full of little cafes, ice cream
parlors and pastry shops. Jews, especially the German Jews, are
famous for their sweet tooth and sitting in a coffee house is an age
old pastime in all of Central Europe from where most of us came.

Mama and I enjoyed our morning coffee breaks together,
but sometimes she just could not get away in the mornings. On those
occasions I took the children downhill near Jaffa Street where my
brother Floh had his carpenter shop. If he was in he could always
spare a few minutes to sit with us for a short while in one of his
favorite haunts for coffee and cake.

If neither Mama nor Floh were free, I usually could convince
one of the many acquaintances that I met on the way to indulge in a
snack and have a chat. By the time Jacob came home for lunch I was
always back home and had lunch ready for him.

Jacob worked only in the morning during the summer
months, except for a few days every month when they had to balance
their accounts. However, he did not spend his afternoons with us.
He had too many friends of his own. He also visited his parents very
often and his father's grocery shop across from the citadel inside of
Jaffa Gate was where his friends could find him.

Usually Jacob was back home for dinner, and whatever we
had planned for the evening. A few times, much to my distress, he
did not come home, but played poker with his friends into the wee
hours of the next morning. I objected violently to this practice. I
had no qualms about playing poker, but I was deeply worried when
he did not come home. I always feared that something had happened
to him.

We found a simple solution to this problem. Most of the
poker games from then on took place in our home. I provided
refreshments, and sometimes joined the game or curled up on a
corner of the couch and read until I fell asleep fully clothed on the
couch. I could not go to bed because we had only one room that
served as dining, living and bed room with hideaway beds. Occa-
sionally I put the table and chairs out in the hall, so that I could go

to bed. Usually I preferred to watch the game or take part in it, although I was quite timid and seldom gambled as high as the men. At the end of many hours of passionate gambling each of them ended up with approximately the same amount of money with which they had started.

Since my office hours were in the afternoon, I usually stayed home until five. When none of my clients showed up, and I was finished with my correspondence, I had time for ironing or baking cakes. I baked at least twice a week because we had so many guests

Sometimes I left in the late afternoon to go to Benediction at the Reparatrice convent, the Sisters of Zion, where I had friends, or in the Church of the Holy Sepulchre. It was a beautiful walk in the late afternoon when it was no longer very hot and the children enjoyed going to the old city.

But the best afternoons we spend on our balcony which I fell in love with when I saw the house for the first time. One of our tenants usually came over for a cup of coffee because she had just finished her day's work in the baby home where she worked or studied. Later we also rented to several couples and whoever lived in one of our rooms was entitled to have coffee with us on the balcony in the late afternoon. This hour, just before sunset, is of incredible peace and beauty in Jerusalem.

We had a panoramic view, the old Mamillah cemetery that is now a municipal garden was neglected and overgrown at that time, but down in the valley was an open pool that glistened in the last rays of the setting sun. Beyond the cemetery were the houses and spires of new Jerusalem on the left, and the city wall and old Jerusalem on the right. Exactly strait across from us rose the Mount of Olives with the spires of the Church of Ascension pointing into the clear sky that was a light purple color at that time of the day. Just before sunset, a deep silence descended upon the city. The noise from the streets seemed muffled, the birds suddenly stopped their songs and a far away music seemed to play. It was as if the music of the spheres was audible to our mortal ears. We stopped our conversation and just looked and listened.

Everybody in Jerusalem who takes the time to stop and listen can hear this music, and can experience the moment of serenity just before sunset, but our house was the ideal place to enjoy this phenomenon.

Jacob and his brother, who worked as interpreter for the British Army, made many friends among the Australians that were stationed in Jerusalem and later we joined a group of Catholic soldiers and civilians, the "Sword of the Spirit". Jacob was in his element when he acted as tourist guide to his new friends, and he brought all of them home to experience our daily moment of beauty and serenity on our balcony. With our friends from the "Sword of the Spirit" we had interesting talks and lovely parties. When we had nothing else to do we went to the movies or a concert. We had plenty of baby sitters and were free to come and go and have many memorable experiences while we lived in the Sekilaridis house.

View facing East with the Mount of Olives in the background,
from the balcony of the house on Sekilaridis street, circa 1965.

Steffi with baby George on the balcony of the Sekilaridis house.

*Mairik with Elizabeth Orfali (Yergatian)
at the entrance of the St. James Church
of the Armenian Convent*

The Orfali family before leaving Brazil to emigrate to the USA.

The Teeth of Polycrates

The cargo ship SS Del Monte ploughed steadily northwards. The calm sea sparkled in the sun. The silvery expanse of the South Atlantic was dotted with little tufts of soapsuds. In the West, the misty coastline of Brazil disintegrated into a formless horizon.

I was lying in a soft-pillowed deck chair, completely relaxed, with my hands folded under my head, contemplating the pleasant monotonous view.

"How are you today, on this wonderful morning, Mrs. Stephanie?" the voice of the first mate, Mr. Douglas, interrupted my reveries.

"I'm feeling wonderful. This is too good to be true. I'm feeling like Polycrates on the roof of his castle."

The story of Polycrates

"And who is this Mr. Polycrates?" asked Mr. Douglas and offered me some chewing gum.

I took it and popped it in my mouth. But it stuck to my partial denture and I had to remove it, while Mr. Douglas sat down on a deck chair next to mine. As soon as he was settled, I began my story.

"Polycrates was in ancient time the tyrant of the Mediterranean Island of Samos. It is an old Greek legend. We German children know the story through a famous poem by the German poet Friedrich Schiller, a poem that nearly all children have to learn by heart. Polycrates stands on the roof of his palace and boasts to his guest, the king of Egypt about his good luck and his happiness. He points to his beautiful island with its fertile field, his many ships in the harbor, he tells about his well-filled treasury. While they stand there, messengers come and announce a victory over his enemies, and the successful return of his fleet, laden with precious goods. The king of Egypt shakes his head. "So much good luck will cause the envy of the gods." He suggests that his host sacrifice something to the gods to appease them. Polycrates is impressed, and with a sweeping gesture, takes off his precious ring and throws it wide out into the sea.

The next day, the cook finds the ring in the stomach of a fish he is preparing for dinner, and takes it back to his master. The king of Egypt who witnesses this scene is deeply shocked. "The gods refuse your sacrifice, this means disaster," he utters, and leaves Samos. The poem ends there, but it implies that a terrible disaster overtook the tyrant."

"That's a nice story, but what has it to do with you?"

Fish on the hook

Just as I prepared to answer, we were interrupted by the buzzing of an alarm clock, The cry "Fish on the hook" was heard all over the ship. We left our seats and ran with everybody else who was not on duty to the stern of the ship where three fishing lines were trailing in the water. A number of sailors hauled in a heavy line. We could see that they fought an enormous foe. Their faces were red and beads of sweat glistened on their foreheads as they pulled, let go, and heaved again. Suddenly, they let go completely, cursing vehemently. The fish had got away. It swam merrily in the water, away from our cooking pots.

Mr. Douglas and I returned to our deck chairs and I needed little encouragement to continue my story.

"You wanted to hear the relation between my story and the famous poem. You know that we have been refugees before we came to Brazil. Our first years in Sao Paulo were extremely hard. The schools for our children were very bad, and I suffered from severe asthma, and bad teeth. Then suddenly, a number of fortunate incidents occurred, one after the other. My asthma got much better with new drugs. We finally saved a little money that we invested in a piece of real estate. Jacob found a new and better paying position with the Sao Paulo Light and Power Company. Then we received a letter from Jacob's long lost aunt, who had become wealthy and invited us to join her in Chicago. She gave us an affidavit of support and sent us the money for the journey.

As if all this good luck were not enough, we found passage on this friendly ship, at such a reasonable fare, where we are treated like royalty. Such a contrast to our passage to Brazil in the third class hold of an emigrant ship. Finally, during the stop of our ship in Victoria, Jacob was able to convert the money from our little piece of land into precious gems at a fraction of their value.

"And now, you are afraid of the jealousy of the gods," chuckled the First Mate.

I nodded solemnly.

"Don't be so superstitious" he said, and have confidence."

We were silent now and stared out into the sunny ocean, mildly aware of our need for nourishment. When the dinner bell finally rang, we left our deck chairs as fast as our dignity permitted and proceeded to the dining room that we shared with the officers.

The table was immaculately set with a shining white table cloth, elegant china, crystal glasses and table silver. My mouth was watering in anticipation of the culinary feast. I took one of the inviting appetizers and put it in my mouth, alas, I could not bite it. "Where were my teeth?"

Then I remembered that I had removed them in order to enjoy the chewing gum.

"Please excuse me," I murmured and left the table to look for my denture.

I looked on the deck chair, under the deck chair, next to the deck chair, on the lower deck, in the bathroom, in our cabin. I looked and looked, but the denture had disappeared without a trace.

I returned to the dining room to eat at least some of the dessert, and to tell my family blushingly about my mishap.

Our son George teased me, "I guess, one of the fishes is now eating your teeth."

All the family helped in the search until we sank exhausted on our beds for a siesta. I had just fallen asleep, when the familiar buzz announced: "Fish on the hook." We dressed quickly and followed the others to the afterdeck.

The line was very heavy. Ten men pulled it. Finally a huge marlin came into sight. More men grasped the line. The fish was now in midair, wriggling desperately to get itself loose. At last, the silvery creature writhed on deck. We all stood back in awed silence as Mr. Douglas stepped forward and flashed a long sharp knife. He neatly slashed the throat of the fish. Blood oozed over the freshly scrubbed deck. After a last effort to leap into the air, the movements of the monster became weaker and weaker until they ceased altogether.

Now, the cameramen went into action to immortalize groups of the crew and us, the only passengers, with the 50 pound plus trophy, that was now hanging head down under the awnings. Finally Mr. Douglas drew his knife again to open the fish. I had already looked into the fish's mouth. It had a nice set of natural teeth, but nothing else. I stood, and held my breath as Mr. Douglas opened the belly of the fish, took out the stomach, and opened it carefully. I heard the grating of hard objects. Could it be? I braced myself to take a good look.

There were small stones and shells in it, but no teeth. The gods had accepted my involuntary sacrifice. Our luck still holds. But for the time being no steaks for me.

Orfali family with First Mate Douglas
the steamship Del Monte on the passage
from Brazil to the US.

*The marlin caught on the Del Monte
during the passage from Brazil to the USA.*

Steffi with the girls from her class in 1962.

How I Became a Teacher

On March 12, 1957 a small tramp steamer coming from Brazil arrived in New Orleans with a cargo of bananas, coffee, carnauba wax and six passengers. We were the passengers my Armenian husband Jacob G. Orfali, our children George 17, Gabrielle 15, Joseph 11, John 6 and me, a German Jewish Refugee. Fate had tossed us over land and seas, and after years in the Middle East and Brazil we looked forward to a home in the United States.

From New Orleans we went to Chicago. Aunt Hozannah, Jacob's aunt whom we had never seen before and who had sponsored and financed our immigration, received us with an open heart and true Armenian hospitality.

The first weeks were bright and promising. Jacob found a good job at Abbott Laboratories in North Chicago. We moved out into the country to Zion, Illinois. We were convinced that we could assimilate ourselves better in a small community where we had to associate with Americans rather than with foreigners. The children had their ups and downs. But they found new friends, mastered the language and adjusted themselves in the new schools. They each have their own story of trials and triumphs.

Mama had to chip in

Jacob's salary, however, was not enough for 6 people. It was the most heartwarming experience to get gifts of furniture and appliances from friends and strangers. But we had to replace these first helter skelter furnishings gradually with more adequate belongings. In consequence, Mama had to chip in. I tried office work. However, the typewriter and I are sworn enemies and my English was still pretty shaky. I lost my job after one single day.

So, I went to work in a curtain factory. Now, sewing curtains isn't so bad. We had a nice crowd of "girls," we had pleasant working conditions even if we were pitifully underpaid. But I got bored stiff sewing those endless seams. I began wondering about how to use all the education I had. I finished 5 semesters of science and chemistry in Germany when Hitler came to power. Then I had to leave the university in a hurry because I was of Jewish ancestry and an officer of the anti-Hitler student's club.

My Quichotic vision

I began to identify with the stuart in the Bible story who buried the talent that his lord had given him. I felt that I had to do something with my abilities. To this end I started a round of letters and interviews with school boards, supervisors, principals, and teachers. The results of my inquiries were rather depressing. I could not teach in American public schools until I was an American citizen, which would not be before March of 1962. The Illinois State Board of Teacher Certification would give me only one year of college credit on my German papers. Nevertheless, I enrolled in a Zion extension course of the National College of Education of Evanston, Illinois.

How I enjoyed the company of the teachers in the course and of our lovable instructor! But I was not yet very sure of myself. Was I like Don Quichote neglecting house and family for run a nebulous scheme that would require years of sacrifice and privations? Daily life at home became more and more problematic. Jacob lost his job during the recession of 1958, and was in and out of work for a considerable time. In the meantime George had graduated from high school and wanted to go to college. We went into debt. It was a hard decision, but I started another course.

My health broke down after the second semester and two years of factory work. I landed in the hospital. The doctor prescribed easier work. I tried another office job which ended in a fiasco after a trial period of 4 weeks. Again, my nemesis, the typewriter did me in. I found myself drawing unemployment checks. I looked half heartedly for another job and I studied with all my heart freshman English in evening courses at the University of Illinois in Waukegan.

Then the unemployment checks ran out. My father was able to send some money from Israel, enough to go on. Now, I really went to work on my studies. Besides taking care of house and family I took 3 evening courses and one correspondence course.

Strange to say, I enjoyed going to school immensely. I got new insights into English, into American heritage and way of thinking, and into American education.

By the end of the spring term 1960, I found out that I could teach in private schools without being American citizen. The minimum requirement was 60 hours of college credits. I was sure I could accomplish this by fall. Everything seemed to be smooth sailing when disaster struck.

I had to have an operation, and as the result of a blood transfusion I got hepatitis. I was on the critical list for a few days. The doctors insisted that I would need all summer for my convalescence.

Thrown into deep water

Was it the result of our prayers or my undying conviction that it was God's will for me to go on? I was able to go to summer school anyway. Then I got a last minute appointment to teach 5th grade in a Catholic school in our vicinity for the academic year 1960-1961.

Though I already had the new textbooks at home, reaching my goal seemed unreal. Then we had our first teachers meeting before school opened and I held the (for me nearly incomprehensible) teacher's handbook and the classroom key in my hands. Reality finally sunk in and I spent the next days in a nightmare of apprehension. How would the children react to my accent? Would they like me? Would I be a good teacher? I spent most of the following days in the classroom, fixing bulletin boards, distributing books and workbooks on the individual desks, and doing paperwork.

The great day finally arrived. Here I sat at my desk while 46 rosy cheeked, scrubbed little angels trooped into the room. The bell rang. I plunged into it. "I am Mrs. Orfali (name on the chalkboard) your new teacher. Let us ask God's blessing for this new school year."

During the first weeks I felt like a person thrown into deep water without knowing how to swim. But I kept floating. I told the children that they could correct my pronunciation, which they did happily but politely. We had a big joke until I could pronounce little Wayne's name without saying "Vane". Everyone in the room learned a lot about dictionary work and the pronunciation key by the time the year was over. As an introduction to geography and map work I told them about my family's travels. The students were very proud of their teacher with the different background.

We had a Teacher's Convention at the end of September. The feeling of "belonging at last" was deeply gratifying. However, new clouds were forming on the home front. My daughter Gabrielle, who was driving me daily to work, went to Massachusetts to Medical Records school. I had to learn to drive myself. After I flunked the driving test the first two tries, I rammed the into a telephone pole on my third try. Now I had to wait one year for a new attempt.

Our son George had to give up college after one year because we didn't have enough money. He was now working in a factory. He began to drive me every morning at 6:15 a.m. to the Northshore Station. From there I took the train and then a bus to school. One nice sunny morning as we drove leisurely and carefree to work, a car charged into us with the force of a mad bull. George's beautiful 1957 Dodge was smashed to pieces and we were sent on an ambulance to the hospital. Luckily we both mended soon. However, George not only lost his car, but was laid off while he was on sick leave. Despondent, he joined the Army and ended up serving Uncle Sam in France.

School went on. Poor Jacob now had to take me to the station before work and to pick me up from school after work.

The teacher learned most of all

The first year of teaching had its drawbacks. Complaints came in about my accent. We had discipline problems with boys who took advantage of my inexperience. I had to feel my way cautiously through class room procedures and test routines. The Sisters and the other lay teachers were as helpful as possible. This first year was nearly over. We had highlights on Christmas when we built a replica of the Village of Bethlehem after my color slides and tales. All the other classes visited our room to see our masterpiece. We published our own magazine of stories and poems and we studied and learned. The teacher learned most of all. I learned the rules of baseball and touch football. I learned American children literature from the children's book reports. I learned American pronunciation from the murmurs when I made a mistake in dictating during a spelling test. We all learned and learned.

Friday before Mother's Day I found a gift box on my desk. It was quite an affair as it happened that the principal was passing by in the hall and came in to see what the commotion was all about. I took a lovely corsage out of the box and a greeting card that said

"To the teacher who treats us like our own mother."

I had tears in my eyes as the Sister pinned the corsage on my dress. It was the crowning of a rich year. Besides school we had all the PTA's, the Cub Scouts, socials and a happy family life.

George hopes to make it to officer's school. Gabrielle is doing fine in Medical Records school. Joseph, now a freshman in high school, has brought a report card of straight A's. Johnny, though his scholastic success is still to come, has at least made the baseball team.

Today, the school children have asked me if anybody is going to flunk. Happily I could reply, "You are all hopping on to the sixth grade, only your teacher is going to repeat the fifth grade."

Steffi the schoolteacher at her desk in the classroom.

Oma Braun's 85th Birthday in 1972, with Orfali and Braun family members.

The Ones That Got Away

The project I envisioned and called "The Ones that Got Away" was never undertaken. However I collected biographies from thirteen friends in a little booklet titled *Our first 60 years*. In the meantime, a survivor from Fürth, Frank Harris, collected biographies from about a thousand former citizens of Nürnberg and Fürth. He organized three grand reunions and several mini-reunions of hundreds of former Nürnbergers and Fürthers. He sends out a yearly newsletter with news of all of us who care to write to him.

During the summer of 1971, I received a fat package in the mail. When I opened it, a number of letters from different sources tumbled out. The first was dated May 1971. It was addressed to four of our former Jewish schoolmates, who went to school with her in Nürnberg in the late nineteen twenties. The letter was written in German. Here is an excerpt in English translation:

"Dear Friends,
Marianne's letter reminded me of the fact, that we will all be 60 years old during the next year. We all have arrived at an age where we understand the importance of the word "health". But it is as important that each of us is busy with something of interest, that gives joy. I hope that each of you has found fulfillment in such a pursuit.
"I will tell you a little about our life. I married in 1937 and we settled in a place without any trees or a house. Together with us came about 30 families. During the next 30 years I was busy raising my three daughters and generations of chickens and goats. The empty place became a village, and in turn became urbanized. It is now like a suburb of Tel Aviv, famous for its beautiful gardens and trees.
"My two eldest daughters are now married and I am a proud grandmother of 7 grandchildren. The eighth is on the way. Ruth, our latecomer studies art in Jerusalem.

"My husband and I like to go to concerts and exhibitions. We like to go on trips, and know our country very well, and are very good tourist guides. We love visitors."This is in short the essence of our lives. I hope to hear from all of you. Again all the best, and greeting to your families.

Yours, Dorle Friedmann, née Bing

I was overjoyed with the letters, read and reread them, and finally wrote a letter to all of them and to other old friends with whom I was still corresponding. The following is a translation of my letter to my friends.

"My dear former school friends,

Marianne sent me letters a while ago from former friends on the occasions of our 60th birthdays. Dorle Friedmann had the great idea to each write a short biography, and to start a chain letter.

We all indulge this year in memories, because of the round number in the years of our lives, and we all have a lot to remember, since our lives were so radically changed when we had to leave Germany.

Sometimes I have to hold my head, and ask myself: "How is this possible?" I the Jewish Steffi Braun with the red hair, from Nürnberg in Bavaria as teacher of French in a Catholic school in Waukegan, Il U.S.A.

With my four children and Armenian husband, I have lived in Israel, Jordan, Lebanon, Brazil, and the United States, had to learn so many foreign languages, (some of you will remember that foreign languages were my weak spot) was ill, and without money so many times, had to go to school again at an advanced age, and have at last found a beautiful home and a modest affluence in Zion, IL 60099. Here we live now and enjoy our children and grandchildren.

Both grandchildren are a mixture of Jewish, Armenian, Italian, Irish and English.

I am sending this letter to all whose addresses I know. Please reply to me by sending short biographies, and the addresses of all whose addresses you know. Write German or English whatever comes easier.

I enclose my Christmas letter, so that you learn a little about our lives. In the meantime, I wait for your reaction.

With best wishes for the next and all further years,

Steffi

I wrote another letter to my school friends explaining that the theme I envisioned for the project was the success we had in overcoming adversity and what we were contributing to society, rather than the suffering of the hollocaust.

My dear Friends,

You may remember that I wrote in my last Christmas letter that I am planning a book *The Ones that Got Away*. The idea for this book came to me when I read the 13 stories that I collected for "Our First 60 Years".

I have been busy the last year with many things, like rewriting my book *The Second Goal* in English and German, doing substitute teaching, traveling, and doing civic volunteer work.

The Ones that Got Away was always on my mind. I have written several attempts for a foreword and part of my own contribution, but I have spoken only to Dora Lanir, whose story can be used as it is, and to Dorle Friedmann who gave me a wonderful article about the way she began to feel Jewish. To each of you other contributors who have not yet written, I want to give you a general idea what the book is going to be.

Since I planned the book, I read two important books about the time of the holocaust. One by Hugo Burkhard *Tanz Mal Jude*, and another by Eric H. Boehm *We Survived*. Both books are about the incredible sufferings and persecutions, about the events we would like to forget and which continue to haunt us. Facts that must be told, because the world should not be allowed to forget the inhumanity that goes hand in hand with dictatorship, whether it is fascist, communist, or military.

But the description of atrocities is not going to be an important part of our book. It has to loom in the background as a menace that must never be allowed to occur again.

Have you done anything in you life that reflects your determination to prevent another break-down of the democratic process? Have you worked in the framework of your life after you left Germany? What was the outcome of your Nazi experience? Like volunteering in World War II, building Israel, joining the peace movement, being active in politics, working against discrimination, doing social work, helping people who are worse off than you?

I know that many of you have helped refugees. Maybe you would have done it anyway, because in Germany, even before the debacle, we were full of social awareness, but most of us got strengthened in our purpose by the persecution which we went through.

So, I want to collect not stories of suffering, but stories about overcoming the result of suffering. In a way all of our stories are success stories, because in spite of the drawbacks in our lives, each of us came out with a satisfying, active life, with new roots, in the country to which we have emigrated.

Steffi

Americans do not realize how hard it is to be uprooted, nor how satisfying it is to start from scratch and prove yourself that you can do it.

I spoke recently at the naturalization ceremony of new immigrants. The new Americans expressed appreciation that I mentioned the hardships, the loneliness and the homesickness of immigrants. The old Americans meanwhile, told me that they never realized how hard it is for immigrants to reroot in a new country.

While writing my first fictional story about our experiences in Brazil, and then my autobiography, I realized something else. I could be a lot more honest in a fictional story than in an autobiography, because I had to leave out many events, experiences and emotions that were too personal, embarrassing to myself or others, to be published, but that might be attributed to a fictional character in a novel.

The reason I want to undertake *The Ones That Got Away* is that I have talked about my plan with numerous people who found it worthwhile, and believed there would be interest and readership for the kind of stories we have to tell.

That is where you come in. You are the ones who have lived the stories. You have come to a new country with nothing more than your education and your memories, and you have found heartbreak and happiness, hard work and leisure, sickness and health.

By the way, one thread runs through all your stories. Although we are all very attached to our new homes, we have become cosmopolitans. We all like to travel, and spend most of our extra cash traveling to know our new country or visiting the old country, or to get to know yet other new worlds.

More about my unfinished project and my opinions:
On January 1, 1974 at an age of 62 I received my first retirement check. I was pregnant with the book *The Ones that Got Away* for a long time. I thought it wanted to be born.

At several periods of my life, I would have started it with a heartfelt prayer for success in my endeavor. God certainly would like me to write this book about man's triumph over forces stronger than the victims of persecution.

But how could God have let these evil forces loose in the first place. How could he permit the slaughter of 6 million Jews, many of them with prayers on their lips. In war, God is assailed with prayers from each of the antagonists. He cannot grant the prayers of both sides unless he gives them peace without a victory. Peace is one thing God cannot give us unless we humans will it.

When we Americans, self-styled torchbearers of liberty bombed helpless women and children in Vietnam who probably prayed as hard for survival as we prayed for "Peace with Honor", I became more confused than ever. What is God's will? Why does the bible tell us to pray, when life shows us its futility? Who am I, to try to change the flow of events by my self-centered prayers?

So, I don't pray any more for my personal concerns. I admire God in his creation. I am grateful for the beautiful planet on which we live, and I shudder at the harm we are doing to it all the time. I try to follow the basic moral requirements of the Golden Rule which is by no means the monopoly of Judeo-Christian teaching, and resign myself to my personal impotency, while trying to work for a better world in my minuscule role.

As I grow older, my earlier life becomes more vivid as the daily life becomes duller. I was lucky to have interested listeners to my stories, while I worked as a substitute teacher during the last year. When the students hear that I am from Germany, their first reaction is: "Tell us about Hitler." It seems that the uncertainty about Hitler's death has an unending magic for them. Hitler is still a memorable figure for many of them, and the Hitler era is still a reality for them, because of the many reruns of World War II films on TV.

I usually get permission to tell the students my stories instead of following the regular program. I tell them about the early years of the Third Reich and the trap into which the German people fell, when they voted for Hitler in a democratic election. I tell them about World War II, about the holocaust of the Jews, and finally about the fate of "The Ones that Got Away".

This summer, I had a wonderful experience, that brought back the past in living color. I was able to spend a week in Germany with my granddaughter. Veronica was an avid listener to my stories, good and bad. We even went together to the former Dachau Concentration Camp, where some of my friends perished.

The Ones That Got Away was never completed, but that is a good description of our family. I got away from Hitler and moved to the Middle East. Then our family got away from the strife in the Middle East when we moved to Brazil. After that we escaped the coup and repression that later overtook Brazil by emigrating to the USA. Finally my husband Jacob and I escaped the cruel winters and hazards of Post Office politics by retiring to California. Living in the lovely Napa Valley, entertaining friends and family from all over the world, we are truly The Ones that got away.

Steffi and Jacob Orfali on their 25th Wedding Anniversary

About Stephanie Orfali

Stephanie Orfali was born Dec. 14, 1911, in Nurenberg, Germany, where she spent her youth until she fled Nazi Germany to Palestine. In 1935 she met her husband Jacob and together with their children they emigrated to Brazil in 1951. The family emigrated to Zion, Illinois, in 1957. Stephanie and her husband retired to Napa in 1979 where they enjoyed the company of many new and old friends.

Stephanie received a Master's Degree in Guidance and Counseling from Roosevelt University in Chicago. For many years she taught in Illinois at Winthrop Harbor and Antioch. She was also a guidance counselor at Holy Child High School in Waukegan, Illinois.

One of her many hobbies was to write short stories. Some of her stories are collected in this volume. She also authored two books. *Second Goal*, a murder mystery set in Sao Paolo Brazil, was published in 1977. *A Jewish Girl in Weimar Republic*, the acclaimed autobiography of her early years was published in 1987.

Mrs. Orfali was a member of the League of Women Voters, the AARP, which she served as president for two years in Zion, Illinois, Hadassa of Vallejo, the Napa City County Library Docents, and the Napa Senior Center where she enjoyed playing bridge. Stephanie Orfali died at the age of 82 on November 23 1994.

Steffi was a positive and energetic person. She had an uncanny knack for turning adversity to advantage. The title *Making Lemonade* was considered when naming this collection of her stories, as a reference to one of her favorite homilies: "When Life Gives You Lemons, Make Lemonade." The title *A Jewish Girl Finds New Roots* was selected as a reference to her prior book *A Jewish Girl in the Weimar Republic*, which received many excellent reviews, and to signify that she went beyond her origins as a Jew in Weimar Germany to diverse places and cultures where she nurtured deep and enduring friendships.